Formula One Racing

The Thrill of Racing

TOM GREVE

Rourke
Publishing LLC
Vero Beach, Florida 32964

www.rourkepublishing.com

PHOTO CREDITS: © Paddy Briggs: page 5; © Julie Lucht: page 6; © 377719031, Gabi Garcia: page 8; © Oskar Schuler: page 9; © Emil Reising: page 10; ©Ford Media-Photo by Bryn Lennon: page 12; © Ford Media - Photo by Clive Mason: page 13; © ARphotography: page 4, 12, 14, 17; © digitalsport: page 16, 20; © Lori Carpenter: page 19; © jaggat: page 2; © Rafa Irusta: page 22

Edited by Jeanne Sturm

Cover design by Tara Raymo
Interior design by Teri Intzegian

Library of Congress Cataloging-in-Publication Data

Greve, Tom.

Formula one racing / Tom Greve.

p. cm. -- (The thrill of racing)

Includes index.

ISBN 978-1-60472-370-0

1. Grand Prix racing--Juvenile literature. 2. Formula One

automobiles--Juvenile literature. I. Title.

GV1029.G75 2009

796.72--dc22

2008011243

Rourke Publishing

www.rourkepublishing.com – rourke@rourkepublishing.com
Post Office Box 3328. Vero Beach. FL 32964

Table of Contents

Speed Thrills

Car racing has thrilled people around the globe for more than a century. Formula One racing, known as F1, involves sleek, open-wheel cars competing in **Grand Prix** races.

In the late 1800s, Europeans began racing automobiles on roads between towns. After World War II, some Grand Prix race teams agreed upon a new set of rules governing the races. These rules constituted a racing **formula**, and the sport became Formula One.

During a race, F1 Cars only get about 3.1 miles (4.9 kilometers) per gallon.

Bernie Ecclestone

Bernie Ecclestone is the president of F1. He has competed in F1, managed drivers, and owned a team. He sold F1's television rights, turning the sport into a billion dollar business.

THE HISTORY OF FORMULA ONE

	1920s - 1930s	1950	1968
	European Grand Prix Motor Racing at Circuits	First World Drivers' Championship is held	Team sponsorship allowed
1894	1946	1958	1978
Grand Prix Racing on open roads in Europe	Formula One rules are agreed upon	First Championship for Constructors	Bernie Ecclestone becomes President of Formula One

F1 Cars

F1 cars are lightweight, **aerodynamic**, and fast. The driver fits inside a tiny cockpit. There are strict race **regulations** governing the car's construction and use.

F1 cars have a low, flat design with wings to create more **downforce**. This prevents cars from flipping.

How fast can the cars go? In 2004, Juan Pablo Montoya averaged 163 **mph** (262 **km/h**) for an entire lap. F1 cars can travel 220 mph (354 km/h) for short distances.

Thrilling Fact

F1 cars, gassed up with a driver inside, weigh only about 1,300 pounds (600 kilograms).

A regular mid-size car weighs more than 3,000 pounds (1,361 kilograms).

You Asked...

How quickly can F1 cars accelerate?

F1 cars are capable of going from 0 to 100 mph (160 km/h) and back to 0 in less than five seconds.

Thrilling Fact

F1 drivers lie back while driving. If they need a drink during the race, they push a button on the steering wheel and water flows through a straw attached to the helmet.

Michael Schumacher is F1's all-time championship leader. He started racing as a child on a kart track in Germany. He claimed seven Drivers' Championships before retiring in 2006. That means in seven different years he finished first or near the top in enough of the Grand Prix races to earn the most points. He earned millions of dollars throughout his racing career, donating much of it to charity.

Michael Schumacher's first win occurred in Belgium just two years after he started racing.

Many F1 drivers from the past remain in the record books for various accomplishments. Juan Manuel Fangio won five Drivers' championships for four different teams in the 1950s, a feat no other driver has accomplished. Jackie Stewart's near-fatal car accident caused him to start a campaign instituting proper safety measures for the drivers and fans.

Alan Prost

Alain Prost, born in France in 1955, began kart racing as a teenager. He joined F1 in 1980 and a year later won the French Grand Prix. He finished his driving career with four F1 Drivers' Championships.

Kimi Raikkonen, Lewis Hamilton, and Fernando Alonso are top current F1 drivers. Many believe they are rising stars in the sport.

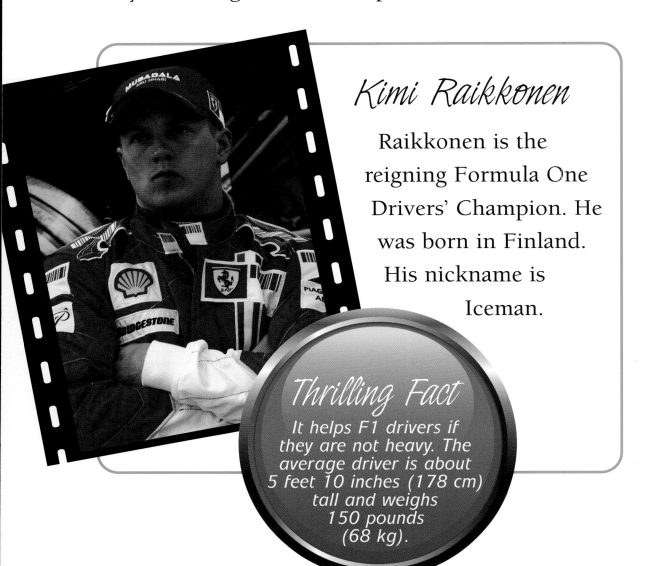

Kimi Raikkonen

Raikkonen is the reigning Formula One Drivers' Champion. He was born in Finland. His nickname is Iceman.

Thrilling Fact

It helps F1 drivers if they are not heavy. The average driver is about 5 feet 10 inches (178 cm) tall and weighs 150 pounds (68 kg).

Big Events

The number of races and even the location of events can change from year to year. In 2008, the schedule includes 18 F1 races in 18 different countries. Drivers race on **circuits** of various lengths and shapes. The drivers go around the circuit in laps until they have traveled 190 miles (305 kilometers).

Countries which host Formula One Races

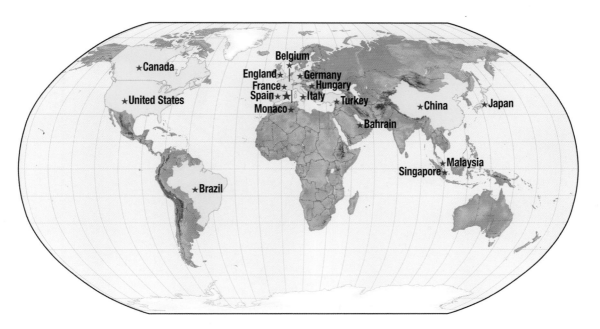

Thrilling Fact

It takes six weeks to set up the Grand Prix of Monaco and three weeks to take it down.

The Grand Prix of Monaco's circuit winds through the streets of Monte Carlo. It is currently the shortest circuit in F1 at 2.1 miles (3.34 km).

The Road to Winning

F1 Grand Prix races are weekend-long affairs. Friday practice sessions let the drivers and teams **adjust** the cars to the circuit. Saturday qualifying sessions determine who gets to race and the order in which drivers will start. Sunday is usually race day.

The top qualifying driver is first in line to start the race. This is the *pole position*.

The cars take warm-up laps before the actual race. They move to their starting spots in the **grid**. Starter lights turn on, then they all turn off, and the race begins. After the race, the top three drivers stand on a podium as the national anthem of the winning driver and team gets played in their honor.

Thrilling Fact

The average F1 driver loses close to 10 pounds during a race. The weight loss is mostly due to the high temperature in the car.

Thrilling Fact

Team Ferrari has won 15 Constructors' Championships, the most of any F1 team.

The top eight drivers and their teams receive points based on the race results. The driver with the most points after the season ends is the Drivers' Champion. The team with the most points is the Constructors' Champion.

Winning involves strategy, perseverance, and luck. Track conditions, the tires, the amount of fuel, and the brakes are all important factors. Pit stops must be quick since lengthy stops hurt the driver's chance to win.

You Asked...

How fast does a pit stop need to be?

It usually takes just 6 to 12 seconds to refuel and change tires.

Pit Crews

Highly skilled teams work quickly during brief pit stops to keep the race cars running at top form during the race. Typical pit stops involve a rapid change of tires and gasoline refill.

The pit is a dangerous spot to work. Race cars sometimes hit workers if a driver misses a signal to stop or accelerate.

F1 is dangerous. Drivers wear helmets and fireproof suits for protection. Drivers also wear a head and neck protector known as the HANS (Head and Neck Support) device.

By wearing a HANS device, a driver's head will not snap forward or back if there is a crash.

F1 uses flags during races to provide safety information to the drivers about the racetrack.

Danger on track, no passing allowed

Hazard cleared, drivers may speed up

03

Driver broke a rule, must go to the pit for penalty, and possible **disqualification**

Warning, driver getting passed by another

Warning, slow vehicle is on the track

Winner has crossed finish line, the race is over

Temporary race stoppage

Engine costs, salaries, and travel add up to make F1 very expensive. Competing can cost a team hundreds of millions of dollars per year. As a result, manufacturers, or major car companies, own the teams.

Thrilling Fact

Big Bucks: Entering a team into F1 requires a $47 million up-front payment. An engine alone can cost more than $100 million per season.

Sponsors get their company name and products displayed on the team's race cars as high profile advertising.

Who pays for all those costs? Sponsors do. In fact, 80 percent of a team's budget comes from its sponsor.

F1 is the fastest and most expensive motor sport in the world. Generations of fans around the globe love the speed and precision of Grand Prix racing.

Glossary

adjust (ad-JUST): make changes

aerodynamic (air-oh-dye-NAM-mik): shaped to reduce drag by moving very easily through the air

circuit (SUR-kit): race tracks for Formula One Grand Prix

constructor (kuhn-STRUHKT-er): F1's term for a team owner

disqualification (diss-kwol-uh-fih-KAY-shuhn): car and driver removed from race for breaking a rule

downforce (DOWN-forss): the pressure of air passing over a moving car pushing the car down so it can make tight turns without flipping

formula (FOR-myu-lah): a model to follow

Grand Prix (GRAND PREE): French term meaning big prizes

grid (GRID): the position of each car at the start of the race

hazard (HAZ-urd): a threat to safety

km/h (KAY-EM-AYCH): abbreviation for kilometers per hour

mph (EM-PEE-AYCH): abbreviation for miles per hour

regulations (reg-yuh-LAY-shuhns): rules and guidelines that teams follow

Index

Websites to Visit

www.formula1.com

http://news.bbc.co.uk/sport1/hi/motorsport/formula_one/default.stm

http://www.fia.com

Further Reading

Herran, Joe, and Thomas, Ron. *Formula One Car Racing.* Facts on File, 2002.

Morganelli, Adrianna. *Formula One.* Crabtree Publishing Company, 2006.

Piehl, Janet. *Formula One Race Cars.* Lerner Publications, 2004.

About the Author

Tom Greve lives in Chicago with his wife Meg. They have two children, Madison and William. He enjoys watching and playing sports, and his hobbies include train travel and bicycle riding.